Complexions Of A Man's Mental
(2nd Edition)

Written By:
Eric McCain

Copyright © 2020

Eric McCain

All rights reserved. No part of this book may be used or reproduced by any means, graphic, electronic, or mechanical, including photocopying, recording, taping or by any information storage retrieval system without the written permission of the publisher except in the case of brief quotations embodied in critical articles and reviews.

Eric McCain books may be ordered through booksellers or by contacting:
Eric McCain
The views expressed in this work are solely those of the author.
Any illustration provided by iStock and such images are being used for illustrative purposes.
Certain stock imagery © iStock.

ISBN: 978-1-64050-401-1

Printed in the United States Of America

The poem that started it all, the first poem I've ever written for the simple sake of creation. I learned about poetry, but never attempted to see what I could do with the art form until creating this in 1998, the year I fell in love with the art. Years later I'm not only still in love, but have fallen even deeper.

Feelings

Feelings are the
    Forever
    Elliptical
    Emotions
    Leveling
        on the
    Inside
        yet
    Never
    Getting
    Said

These pages contain my feelings, some private and some public, but regardless of which, they are finally being said. I pray these words inspire you to invest in your future, believe in, create & recreate yourself. No one will be as effective in any of those categories as you will be for yourself. A good friend once told me that sometimes you have to be selfish in order to become selfless.

From my pencil to your heart,
Eric McCain

Dedication

This book is dedicated to my legacy, my children. To encourage them to reach for Pluto and the galaxies beyond it and walk on their terrain creating new paths for exploration and discovery. To reach for the improbable and the impossible and make it the very opposite. To reach for their dreams and no matter if success or failure is the result they tried, they reached, they created, and they gave and that is what life is all about, creation and giving.

This book is also dedicated to the moments of screaming silence. The moments when your life, the life of others & everything around you is hectic and the only silence or calm you have is that of your thoughts.

Content Of Complexions

Complexion 1 ~ Diction

Cerebral, Verbose

1) Poetical Exercise
2) Je Ne Sais Quoi
3) Clouds Of Uncertainty
4) The Tween
5) Allure
6) For The Men
7) Single Dad, but Who Is He Really
   (describing a moment @ Cobblestone Dr.)
8) Pain
9) Poetry Is A Muthafucka

Complexion 2 ~ Brotha 2 Da Nyght

Reflective, Dark, Religious, Political

1) Dear God
2) Darkness Falls
3) The Art Of Hating Myself
4) A Man
5) Politics As Usual
6) No Problem
7) Storm America
8) Tired

Complexion 3 ~ Pure Titan

*Narcissistic, Confidant, Outspoken)

1) Welcome

2) Imaginary Poet

3) Your Swag

4) One Page

5) Venting

6) Barhead Geese

7) Risky

8) I Love Being A Poet

Complexion 4 ~ Syne

Erotic, Intimate, Sensual

1) Anytime Anyplace

2) Chocolatey Thoughts

3) Stormy Weather

4) Real thing - Wish Granted

5) Desire & Confess

6) Frustration

7) Since You Say I May, You Know I Will

8) You Have One Job

Complexion 1

Diction

"My thoughts build tracks around planets
so I can think outside my own realm"

Poetical Exercise

They call me Diction, because I make words make
    cents,I meant to say sense, since I've become
    the Shogun of the 26 dimensions that connect
    thee entire literary world
I've become the anatomical metaphorically correct
    incarnate of personification, so I reincarnated
    myself as a definition to define myself as what
    defines definition
My swag is impenetrably impeccable
    with no plausible deniability, even when asking
    if swag is a liability
So while no one on the corner got swag like him,
    you're still wondering and guessing
    how I have ample swag to lend

My words talk death to life in reverse
    so they speak life to death
    and have infinite conversations spoken off
    one breath
One breath I breathe, I breathe life to words,
    reborn countless times so the Phoenix is heard
    but what's heard is my middle name

See my last name is Ptolemous, first name's Eraticus
    and I be eradicating irrational mindsets
Mind sex is what I give them,
    massaging and caressing their cerebral
    hemispheres with metaphors & similes,
    haiku & sonnets
Giving them sensory overloads, but they can never
    get enough of a literary gladiator
    verbally mutilating & decapitating
    any and all opponents who oppose my prose
Personification is my weapon of choice,
    but I keep a semicolon like Powell
    on my hip in case I have to face the ghost
    of my past-participles and hopefully
    I won't have to catch a homonym
Are you not entertained?
Are you not entertained?
Is this not why you are here?
Well I wrote this sitting on an all white oxymoranated
    stead named death who lives for eternity
    until I take my last step & with him on my side
    I'm the captain of the calvary
    so that makes me the word play king
    and you don't really wanna scrabble with me!

Je Ne Sais Quoi

Focused on the now not thinking about the how or the why, only the why nots and my girl think I'm bitching… smh

My man Austin calls it mojo, the old heads call it
    libido, the French call it Je ne sais quoi, hell
    some people even call it, IT,
    but me I just call it my shit and I lost it and I
    really need it back
My walk, my talk, & more importantly my very allure
    depends on my quest to reestablish myself as
    myself and get back to being me you see at
    100% my sheer will power can crumble
    mountains and bring conquerors to their knees
My thoughts build tracks around planets
    so I can think outside of my own realm
    fuck a box unless it's Pandora's
    and without a problem I'll open it up
    and release her aurora
All locked up, but my shit is key
    lost and not yet found seems to be my destiny

The sisters of fate dangle my thread in my face
wanting me to cut life short on my end,
but my thread remains strong, no breaks
or bends
Yet I'm focused on the now not thinking about the how
or the why only the why nots and my girl think
I'm bitching… smh

Things are falling apart while simultaneously coming
together, a prosperous future is on the horizon,
but the present is a scornful bitch I fucked over
in my past story now she's back with a
vengeance & flames of hell's fury
Got me on my Arnold shit constantly telling myself
that I'll be back, but I'm scared cause I'm
drowning and 6'1" isn't tall enough to withstand
this ocean of emotions, where I think I lost my
shit
Fear, confusion and anger are hindering my vision
while cloaked around me as if they were
tailored to fit like a three-piece suit, though I
can make anything look good, it's just not a
good look

No emotions on my sleeve I'm not an open book,
    I keep it locked inside cause men always say
    that big boys don't cry so at an early age
    I committed emotional suicide
Now I try to maintain always on the verge
    of going insane in the membrane,
    because these feelings I can't handle
Along time ago I placed my heart on a mantle,
    now I'm trying to get it back and as a grown
    man towards the simple things I know not
    how to act damn, I need my shit back.

Clouds Of Uncertainty

The pressure is mounting as the day goes on...

At this point my maybe baby is here in the world
    life in her limbs, breath in her lungs,
    and a name to be remembered throughout the
    ages... SAIGE

This process is foreign to me
    not being involved and living in the shadow
    of doubt and uncertainty
Prepared to be a father again, returning to the starting
    blocks while maintaining my position at the
    finish line cheering and coaching my first born
    to the end of the race

A daughter... her daughter... my daughter..?
    our daughter..?

Only thing that is known for sure
    is that nothing is known for sure except sex
    and a name

Saige is as beautiful as the name written on this page
    and I have yet to see her or claim her for that
    matter, publicly anyway, privately she's been
    my princess since day one
    or at least that's how I processed it to prepare
    me for today

I'm so torn between love and betrayal...

The love I feel for a child, a daughter,
    though I've never laid eyes nor swab to solidify
    my involvement
The betrayal I fell for myself
    leaving my unborn daughter in the care of a
    woman I barely know and for missing out on
    the process of witnessing her grow

But how could I when her mother and I
    were nothing more than moments in the
    midnight hours, though they were filled with
    pools full of liquor and we caught multiple
    flights the destination was always the same
    and there were no layovers

If my hand was in the cookie jar you would know
> one thing, I'd take the cookie and not leave
> my ring, but this time it was a pack and my
> greed wanted to ransack, taking everything,
> but it was too much to hold and with each
> return flight I became more bold

Some nights taking two or three
> until that fateful night I left a piece of me...
> my ring

Though the day is here
> and Saige is more than a picture
> or a name on a page

This cloud of uncertainty will linger for some moments
> longer, because I need to know if our bond
> is stronger, one between a father and a
> daughter

The Tween

My reality is a living hell I brought upon myself
    I've known lost love, I've have minuscule
    money and now the looming overcast of an
    unborn child
Mommas baby, poppas maybe, but if it's poppas baby
    there is no maybe only a guarantee
    that the day will transform no optimist prime
    from darkness to shine of light
    and she will become my princess,
    even though in actuality she already is

Keep the drink, but pass me a dutchy to the left
    and say it'll be ok in fact keep yours
    I brought my own grassy knoll to Marilyn
    Monroll, attempting to smoke out this 63'
    Chevrolet like I'm JFK, but it's a convertible top
    and no matter how hard I try to convert my pain
    to smoke it still hurts, but persistence has
    got me this far so I take another toke...
    puff puff inhale no passing, this is a
    personal party

I'm the president of my situation & the master of
    my universe, yet a slave to this world and
    its anguish, the hearts I've broken and the
    lives I've ruined
I'd give the air from my lungs for another chance,
    but who would be here to ensure the safety
    and survival of my legacy, my princess and
    my prince, so I'm trapped here, left to straddle
    this fence between heaven & hell, and
    though I'm living in the latter I'll call it purgatory
    as the place that I dwell

The saying goes no pain no gain,
    but I haven't gained shit but more;
    more stress, more heartache, more anxiety,
    more hurt & to make it subside I flirt
    with the woman with the shortest skirt I can find
    so I can manipulate her mind and make
    her mine, but only for one night because I only
    brought enough for us to take one flight and
    although it's a round trip, I pick the destination
    which is straight to ecstasy and straight back
Even if six flags were thrown on the play
    there's no stopping the ride,

so live in the eternity of the moment &
meet your death, it only takes 8 seconds,
eternity in reverse I guess that's why they say
sex is a weapon... BANG!

Call me the Punisher, but this is no movie, there is
    no script, there is no reason to ask whose line
    is it anyway, because it is always mine
I am the leading actor & director,
    never submitting, but always willing to be
    the smith, creating new foundations like
    horseshoes for good luck, yet they always
    seem to get trampled on.
My reality is a living hell I brought upon myself,
    but not only do I live, I thrive in this place
I am the commander & chief of the titanic
    sailing blindly into the glacier filled waters,
    praying for a different outcome,
    but I questioned If God hears me... Déjà vu.

Allure

If I could, I would
If I were able, it would be done
If my time permitted it, I would allow it
If there were more hours in a day
>I would spend them all on her
>and the pursuit of her smile,
>that dazzling, bright as a trillion watt light bulb,
>or zillion karat diamond, stop a man in his
>tracks, stand the earth still on its axis smile

Passing moments of stolen glances frozen
>in messages even though she's not in my
>presence I still find myself slyly capturing
>mental pictures of her physical

Taking her all in daydreaming about her taking me
>all in, but as slaves to this clock that's where
>the daze stops, at dreams until the gravity of
>our reality is weighed and put into play

She's so close, yet I barely know she's around if my
>eyes aren't closed, searching, trying to detect
>the connection in my head that we share

She made Tiffany blue a favorite hue on my list of
    schemes, cause when I lay down and dream
    I play out the scene, of her above me locked
    in a gaze and me being below her transfixed in
    a daze, barely more than silhouettes as we
    peer through a haze exploring each other's
    eyes as if lost in a maze and the contact is
    inevitable, though none is made... yet

I think I see her around yet question
    if it is just my imagination running away with
    me, because a vision of beauty is what stands
    before me and from the looks of things I'd say
    she's for me
When we speak I don't lead just go to where I'm lead
    and through pictures we trade casually
    flirtatious smiles instead
Though the understood needs not to be said,
    I find it invigorating to verbalize the thoughts in
    my head
If I could I would
If I were able to, it would be done
If my time permitted it, I would allow it
If there were more hours in a day,

I would dedicate all of them to her
    and the pursuit of her mind,
    that incredible, sharp as a tack,
    solid a steel trap, empire creating,
    beautiful mind
So if it were possible I'd make her mine

For The Men

This is for the men
The ones who live, love, cry, and willing to die for
    their children
Yes this, is for the men
The ones who can afford the best money can buy for
    their children and the ones who have nothing
    but time to give to their children
For the ones who are willing to sacrifice it all
    to ensure the longevity of their legacy
Yes, this is for you

This is for the men
For the ones who unselfishly play their roles in their
    children lives
For the men who are turned down, turned away,
    and chastised for wanting nothing more than to
    be involved in the process of raising a child,
    their child
Yes, this is for you

This is for the men
For the ones who hold it down and handle business,

bearing the world's weight,
yet continue to strive to be not only great
fathers, but nurturers, and teachers as well
For the men who work holidays and all,
sacrificing their good days
to ensure that their children have great ones
For the men who do all that they have to,
need to, suppose to, and more importantly
want to for their children, yet still are fighting
custody battles and paying support to their
bitter, spiteful, ungrateful ass baby moms
and instead of going from 0-100 real quick
and choking a bitch they deal
Continuing to grind despite the time that passes
between them seeing their children
Yes, this is for you

This is for the men
For the ones who are and have raised their little boys
to become men and teaching them the values
of life and the beauty of chivalry
For the ones who are and have raised their little girls
to become women treating them like
princesses who will become someone's Queen

Showing them how to be loved and teaching them
　　that self-respect and intelligence will take them
　　further than any man, dance, or amount of
　　money can.
Yes, this is for you

This is for the men
For the ones who despite not creating them
　　are willing to raise, ensure the safety of,
　　and impart knowledge to another males
　　children, because of the love that man has for
　　their mother
For the fathers, step fathers, single dads,
　　grandfathers, uncles, brothers, and male
　　cousins who put aside their pride and are
　　willing to humiliate themselves for the
　　betterment of their children
Yes, this is for you

This is for the men
From a man who knows the struggles of what it is to
　　be a father
I COMMEND, RESPECT, & SALUTE YOU ALL

Single Dad, but Who Is He Really
(Describing A Moment @ Cobblestone Dr.)

Legs crossed in chair surfing on a cloud,
    thinking about my life in the sense of the
    why's and the how's
Feeling down on myself, but feeling thankful
    searching for understanding like why has God
    set it up this way or give me such poor lack of
    planning
My mind was so wrapped up in this knot of perplexed
    thoughts and situations, I didn't realize I never
    had the conversation, now it came as elation
    an overwhelming sensation that wrapped me
    so tight it could only be GOD in my foresight
So I said Thank You!

I said thank you for blessing me with another gift,
    I create life, baby girl #2 Kendall Skye is her
    name and though she needs to have my last,
    I'm cool for now because the situation with her
    mom is a thing of the past that my present can
    barely carry

The pressure on my levees is way too heavy,
> they're busting at the seams I'm praying it's all
> a dream, but I know that it isn't

My spark is fading so fast
> I question if I could ever feel warmth from its
> light and my plane just stalled out so I'm
> searching for my light to spark the ignition on
> this flight and continue my elevation although
> the gps is blank, high is my current destination

So I'm smoking and I'm drinking
> and every shot I take compounds the last,
> but the pain is becoming greater
> and my lows are getting lower
> so I finish another, take a toke
> and blow out the smoke in its place
> trying to see my life through the fog filled glass
> and all I see is fog

My head is filled with the screams of broken promises
> I made to myself and shattered dreams
> that the pieces have broken into
> unrecognizable fragments or they're stealth,
> because I can no longer see them

Time is ticking & reality is looming,
    waiting right outside the door
    conversing with her comrades,
    telling the cold to seduce my soul
    and the sobering winds to not give in
    until my spirit is broken and my will is too weak
    to do anything but become a token of my
    societal influences
A product of my environment, trapped in the black
    hole that is my city with more potential than ten
    poets, but on a path that will lead no one to
    ever know it
Reality is a bitch

My prince is my saving grace,
    my sanity in a world that is so crazy
    God's tears can no longer wash away its
    lunacy
I'm teaching him to be a man, thee man
    while learning the same lessons from him
My two princesses increase my crazy,
    but three kids should push me way past lazy
It's hard when I have a stable of thoroughbreds
    that keep me fed, and don't require to be wed,

but are more than willing to give me head
and let me take them to bed
so with that being said,
beautiful distractions should be motivation
I can thank them for their service to my craft
by creating a dedication
so to every honey I played and heart I slayed
that keeps me paranoid to this day...
I'm sorry!

Nowadays my reflection shape shifts
into various versions of the original image
I look in the mirror & sometimes I'm Freddy C,
an incarnate of nightmares & greatest fears,
but that's not really me so as I shake off the
visual and fight back the tears
Other times I'm Freddy P
you see there's a certain allure about me,
females can't deny so turn off the lights & light
a candle now the real me can hide behind a
façade of not lies, but a bit of truth bends,
an endless cycle I'm addicted to so I can't see
the end

A single father, a lady's man, an entrepreneur,
>   a writer, a poet, an artist, a friend, a brother,
>   a confidant, a lover, a shoulder to cry on,
>   an ear to listen, a strong man, a powerful
>   presence, a shy guy, and a plethora of other
>   things

So who is he really, who am I?
I am all of thee above,
>   constantly changing & evolving
>   trying to earn my wings so I can fly

Now my flight is over,
>   no more tokes to take, so I pack up my things
>   and take these thoughts with me, knowing I am
>   a man preparing myself for what the day brings

Pain

If there was ever a moment she questioned my love
    I would die just to make it to the heavens above
    and ask God for a personal favor,
    that he'll keep my soul now
    so if hers ever meets danger it will save her
The hardest part of loving is knowing
    when to let go, my mind says yes,
    but my heart acted as if it did know
Ignorant to the fact that she's leaving me behind
    for bigger and better things, she is off to find
Never consulting me at all,
    yet bringing it to my attention late
    because she was trying to stall
    knowing my heart would fall into an abysmal pit
    with my spirit and mind following, man
    I HATE THIS SHIT
No love lost though, no hate nor strife,
    and I can't say those years were wasted,
    because every second of everyday with you
    changed my life

I've grown & matured and I thank her for that,
    but waiting is something I couldn't do
    and that was the simplest of facts
I had to many places to go,
    so many things to see
    and to be honest a lot of ladies
    had been checking for me
I paid them no mind and threw on the blockers
    knowing the hills have eyes and there were
    always a plethora of watchers
But I was a man with pride,
    so you don't do shit like that
    you don't pick up and leave
    and leave me sick like that
My man Hov said best
    so I had to quote it
    and so my highs balance my lows
    the bud I tote it, twirling them back to back
    so the first dutch I cracked
    was to alleviate the pain
    and the second one is to elevate my brain,
    but when I came down it all remained the same
God please,
    relieve me of this pain

Complexion 2

Brotha 2 Da Nyght

"My only prayer is that me not being the devil incarnate, but merely his advocate does not mean my son is destined to the same fate as me"

Dear God

I have some questions on my mind
    and if you have the time I need some help
    to understand some things that are bothering
    me, affecting my growth in becoming the man,
    that I want to be whole heartedly I pray you see
    the good and continue to believe in me

I was told to pray & leave it all in your hands,
    but that's contradictory, because what was also
    instilled in me says passing on my burdens
    makes me less of a man
So I bare the weight... just call me Atlas

I hope we can get past this miscommunication,
    this misunderstanding because it's tough
    to hop on a plane and trust you'll handle the
    landing, yet I fly & I trust

I'm striving for perfection while avoiding becoming
    lame, but I don't see change, the things I need
    to stop, well they all remain the same

I keep a constant dialogue with you throughout my
    day, but with the very same breath
    there are curses in the things I say
Sinning is so easy, it all comes natural
    the wrong things feel right
    and the right seems un factual,
    but the devil is a lie
If I live by your will I'll learn to let the evil subside
I hate being misunderstood,
    yet could care less if people understand,
    they say ignorance is bliss & this is a peaceful
    land
I ask questions, yet already have the answers
    and I'm sure that leaves you fuming, but being
    simply complex is what makes us all human
It is said that the hardest question to answer is
    "who are you?" Well I know I am a man of God,
I just pray that it's true

Darkness Falls

My mind is being crushed,
    I'm on the verge of a conniption
My nonexistent third eye senses
    the nearing apocalyptic transience
    looming on the visages of the future
My heart transpires with the Devil
    while GOD illuminates himself
    unto my soul
My very own Déjà vu experience,
    trapped within an ellipse
    of constant spellbinding torture,
    though I'm immune to the pain

My time is shortened
    as eternity escapes from my lips
    with every curse that is spoken
My words speak death to life and
    life to nothingness as I am damned
    to live with the gift & curse
    of a fluent tongue
My unnatural ability of speech
    leads me straight to the gates

that lack the pearly luster we all dream to see,
and straight to the ones that glow with a dark
aura of trapped souls, doomed to relive their
sins throughout all of eternity

My demonic eyes represent
    my intentions with life
    and just how deep the darkness
    has burrowed into my heart
My charm has been
    referred to as devilish,
    so I wonder if that's mere coincidence
    or I'm not alone with my gift
    of seeing a person for who they really are

My only prayer
    is that me not being the devil incarnate,
    but merely his advocate
    does not mean my son is destined
    to the same fate as me
The sins of the father
    resulting in the child having to pay

The Art Of Hating Myself

I say I love you,
    but how can I mean it,
    when I'm a cheating bastard
I am a liar
    a denier
    a conniver
    a deceiver
    a master manipulator
    and above all else
I am thee Illusionist,
    a king of perception,
    making everything that was
    seem as though it wasn't,
    everything that is
    seem as though it isn't
    and everything that could have been
    seem as though it was never even a possibility
My covert mission
    is to gain your trust,
    win your heart,
    then tear it out with my bare-hands
    right after I leave the side of another woman

I am savage
> heartless
> cold-blooded
> and above all else

I have no conscious
> allowing me to crush hopes,
> destroy dreams,
> and obliterate hearts
> without a blink
> without flinching
> without any remorse,
> nor regret

I am a disease
I am a plague
I am the anatomically super correct
> human reincarnate of the bubonic
> with an inner core blacker than myself

Talking is 1st on my list of attributes,
> as I have a tongue capable of producing words
> equivalent to thee fallen angel's musical talent

With the smart ones,
> I am smarter

With the witty ones,
> I have more wit

With the ones who aren't so quick on the draw,
> I take pure advantage

With the ones who think they are players,
> I am the play

With the ones who like to play games,
> I am the game

With the ones who are out for revenge,
> I am Freddy Cruguer

With the ones who think like a woman and act like a
> man, I am the deconstruction of that blueprint

Sex is 2nd on my list of attributes,
> as I am the physical manifestation of pleasure

My porn star type talents takes them to another plane
> allowing them to reach immense orgasmic
> heights with each passionate session

I leave them feeling good,
> they make me breakfast and I'm off to either
> prepare or hunt down my next prey

I am thee Predator

I am man

I am strong

I am a vindictive tyrant
> bent on total heart domination

I have no match, no equal

I am weak

I am a scared boy

I suffer from a broken heart,
        due to lost love,

YES, I once knew love

There was a time
        when I had a heart that was vibrant
        and pumping red blood, but it was pierced
        and left a withered shell of a love organ

I say I love you
        and I want to mean it

I don't want to be a cheating bastard

A Man

I am not that scornful feeling
    that was welded into your pride
I am not the fury
    that burns within your eternal soul, that the
    white darkness has embedded within you
I am not that insane, irrational, disfigured emotion
    buried far beneath the depths
    of your entire non-celestial being,
    sending a bombardment of subliminal shots
    to your spirit-man

The perception you have of me
    is the everlasting visual feeling that you've
    been yearning and craving for
I am so intoxicating
    that it causes you to rethink and question
    yourself if you really want to cast me
Though you would wish for me
    to please you
    enchant you
    embrace you,
    and admire you

I am illuminated unto you
      and yet though I do not enchant you
      nor charm you
      you still dream about me
      and want me,
      yet you should not lust for me

Be not forgetful,
      I am more than merely a man
I am the creator of all
      including you and still you must & will have me
Even as I do not morph self,
      yet remain all powerful
      throughout the ages

I am genuine towards you
      notice you and always respect you,
      wiped tears from your eyes, stood up for you,
      and blocked the slander of others
My wisdom has graced you
      remembered you
I lift you up
      you slip into bliss

I am not that scornful feeling
    that was welded into your pride
Bliss guides you to reach such a conclusion
    you would've lead a life of no pain
    had the originals not messed Up

You need not to search any longer
    as your origin, goal, purpose, and destiny
    are within the confines of my hands
I am a being too radiant
    for you to glare upon
    and even as I rebuild you
    reconstructing your inner passion
You rise from amongst the ashes
    acquiring wings of fire & knowledge
    that carry you a flight

Protocol son is what you are
    as you return to who originally made you
    with the heart of David
    and the obedience of Abraham
You can't forget me
I am the Czar of your techni-color imagination
    not only the essence,

but the essential bod of thee ultimate king
with a heart, and a mind
overflowing with love that cannot be measured
the one true teacher

You are a mold
    derived from the mud of the earth
    not born,
    but created in my image
    and while I remain
Elohim — I Am That I Am
El-Shaddai — God Almighty
Adonai — Your Lord
Jehovah-jireh — Your Faithful Provider
Jehovah-rohpe — Your Healer
Jehovah-nissi. — Your Banner
Jehovah-M'Kaddesh — Your Sanctification
Jehovah-shalom — Your Lord of Peace
Jehovah-tsidkenu — Your Lord of Righteousness
Jehovah-rohi — Your Loving Shepherd
Jehovah-shammah — Ever Present With You
    and through all this, you remain a man

Politics As Usual

Change, thee inevitable force of life
    the only thing that regardless of
    how much we fight, it's gon' happen
Change gon' come
    and that's word to Sam Cooke,
    we are not too far from the days
    when it was said,
    "if you wanna hide something from a black
    person just put it in a book, I bet they won't
    look."
Just like Sam Cooke we have the ability to be
    the catalyst for your conscious,
    the difference maker
    the spark in the dark lighting the way
    to change and new liberties
I'm tired of hearing people say,
    "my vote doesn't count anyway,
    I'll let things take their course, tomorrow's a
    new day."
Now I get that you're just one person,
    one citizen in the crowd, but it's your God given
    right to vote and make your country proud

If not your country then your state,
    in fact, I'm sure you can relate
    if I say neighborhood, it's not all good
    when you think about the things
    that's happening in the hood

Listen to what Langston said,
    "I don't want my freedom when I'm dead,
    I can't eat off tomorrow's bread."
Neither can you, neither can we
    cause tomorrow's not promised
RIP Michael Brown, Eric Garner, Ezell Ford, John
    Crawford, four unarmed men killed by police
    and there's no clear cut answer to when the
    violence is gon' cease, so as you read this
    piece allow me to speak my peace

We are more than a hashtag society,
    intelligent enough to speak on the topics
    that aren't trending rather than just sit quietly
Dedicated to do the work, no matter how much it
    hurts, things gon' get done yes change gon'
    come, but ignorance isn't bliss
History proves that to make these moves intelligence

and capital will be required not just a closed fist
So if you should fail to cast your vote,
> then you cannot complain, about the choices
> made nor the prices paid

Yes, you must refrain,
> because political awareness you did not
> promote and your rights you choose to abstain

May the ones we vote for be worthy of our trust
> and pledge on their honor
> to do the things that are just,
> and strive to make a difference
> as they serve faithfully
> to protect the rights of both you and me...

VOTE!

No Problem!

I do not have a problem
I repeat, I do not have a problem
I mean yeah
    I am a deceiver
    I am a liar
    I am a denier and
    I am a conniver, but
I do not have a problem
    and no I'm not trying to come up with excuses,
    because I really do realize that my mindset is
    ruthless... No!
I do not have a problem
    and besides excuse is such an ugly harsh
    word, I prefer intellectually evasive comments,
    that start with "see, the situation with that is,"
    or "what had happened was," or better yet
    "there was this one time at band camp"

So you see I not only do not have,
    but I cannot not have a problem
If I indeed did have a problem,
    my problem would be that you're concerned

with my so called problem, so if anyone you're the one with the problem and I don't appreciate you trying to off your problem as my problem, so I revert back to my previous statement that says, I do not have a problem!

I mean yeah
    I party
    I smoke
    and I drink,
    but for one minute don't think
    that I don't love the lord,
I mean I'll give him a praisedeluijah
    just as fast as the next man,
    so you see that I do not have a problem!

I pray all the time,
    I thank him for blessing me
    and I ask him for stuff,
    but I do all I can, I can't do no more
    because times be rough
Yeah maybe I could
    squeeze in a couple more services,
    but see the situation with that is,

    my schedule it be hectic and I be busy and
Yeah maybe I could have a stronger prayer life,
    but, see what had happened was
    my momma and grandmamma pray for me
    and they are warriors so I can live off their
    prayers for the next 5...10...15 years and
Yeah maybe I could take the opportunities
    I have to witness to actually witness,
    but see there was this one time at band camp
    and I approached a fellow real cool and
    humble and the next thing I knew the bull Qua
    wanted to rumble and things got out of hand,
    but to make a long story short
I do not have a problem

Like I said none of these are excuses,
    they are simply intellectually evasive
    and please don't think that I'm coming off
    abrasive, but it's so much easier to stay where
    I'm at, because I'm comfortable
It's easy to do the things I do,
    go the places I go,
    say the things I say,
    and rock the way I rock

because when I look at the clock
I got plenty of time or do I?
Yeah I have time to come around
because by the time the horn blows
and the sky cracks I'll basically be in the
ground and I'll have had the chance to live my
life fully the way I wanted to live it
so there was never a reason to fully submit it
or was there?
Yeah I have time,
because even though they say these are the
last days, they've been the last days since the
last days been the last days, so I figured I have
a few more days or years or do I?
So I am going to continue to be intellectually evasive
and I am going to a continue to be
a deceiver
a liar
a denier and
a conniver
I am going to continue
to party, to smoke and to drink
because I DO NOT HAVE A PROBLEM
or do I?

Storm America

How will we survive in America
    when it is not set up for blacks
I'd rather be euthanized instead of this genocide
    and with these puppets as our president
    who will have our backs
Americas flow is blood & tears instead of milk &
    honey and what is valued over black human
    life unfortunately, is money
Land of the free & home of the brave
    more like sea of injustice to keep us enslaved
There are two Americas,
    there is one for the whites and the other
    wouldn't allow the whites to sleep at night
It's like a nightmare on Elm St.
    we can't wake up from,
    but our minds shine like Optimus Prime
    with the matrix of leadership
    makings us monarchs before our time
They do not just contain athletics
    there is knowledge, power, and wisdom
    infused in our genetics

So let this be a lesson,
        to embrace our blackness
        because we will never be scared of ya,
        just know that this is the prelude
        of us storming america

Tired

There were moments where I grew tired of being
    a poet, tired of being charged with this charge
    of being one of the guardians of the gate
Protecting the very fabric of even these lines
    I've written for you, but from who
The masses of people of who don't even know
    the difference between there, their, and they're?
So as they sit there wondering where their next like
    is coming from they're missing out on the best
    parts of life, which is human connection
It's like I'm standing in a crowded space with no one
    who cares and of that no one even fewer are
    real
There is no originality they are all robotic clones
    masquerading as humans as if no one can tell
    the difference, I can, but I don't give a fuck
My presence and style makes me one of the first to
    be noticed, yet I'm the last to speak, but often
    the first to make a move
Being a silver tongue is a gift,
    but the females call it a blessing and me a God,
    I've heard them both and some

These days if I make an attempt I'm satisfied
>   unbeknownst to the masses I've accomplished
>   more than 10 men when women are involved

But are they truly accomplishments
>   or notches on a make believe belt
>   making me the champ of a game
>   I've been playing by myself since I bust my first
>   nut

So what's next where will the next conquest come
>   from, I am searching for passion and a thrill that
>   can rival being a conqueror taking a female's
>   mind and body, yet leaving her spirit for God

because I have no use for it

Complexion 3

Pure Titan

"My complexities are so mental
that them creating a ripple in time is common,
since the sense of my mind isn't so common
I haven't been writing like I've got common
sense."

Welcome

I have made movements in time,
    while basking in the stillness of the moment
I try to avoid the inevitable,
    yet often pursuing the questionable
Resisting good wholesomeness leaves behind a bitter
    taste while giving into temptation is always so
    sweet
The battle of mental complexities rage
    while the calm waters of common sense
    reveals not even a ripple
My complexities are so mental
    that them creating a ripple in time is common
    since the sense of my mind isn't so common
    I haven't been writing like I've got common
    sense
Thus the rage continues

Attempting to understand an enigma
    that precedes the existence of that very
    enigma that is attempted to be understood is
    futile
That enigma is me

Women say they don't understand me
    my logic is off, my reasoning is deferred like
    that of Langstons dream, and my situation
    interpretation is like that of an infinitely
    answered sudoko number puzzle and there are
    too many possible scenarios and alternate
    routes to reach an ultimately inevitable answer

The ignorant public watch the movie that is my life
    with a prejudge mental, unbelieving as to how
    comfortable I seem to be and how I
    nonchalantly continue to be a mystery
    and avoid letting any female get too close
Unknowing to them I have been doomed
    to suffer the same fate as Atlas
Cursed to bare the weight of my world
    on my back and broad shoulders
The same world I've brought so much pain in
The same world I've caused so much heartache in
The same world I've created so much pleasure in
The same world I've been placed on a pedestal in

So does that make me a TITAN
    amongst this world?

A higher being forged within the flames of Olympus
    and given life by the lightning of Zeus?
Thus giving me an unfair advantage over
    the mere mortals of this world, allowing me to;
    out think any critical thinker
    out talk any philosopher
    out maneuver any strategist
    and stay three steps ahead of any woman
Well if so I have just been formally introduced
    to who the masses of my friends, peers and
    associates know, and he is the entity known as
    Mr. Eric "Pure Titan" McCain
Hello and welcome to my world

Imaginary Poet

I gotta be one of the dopest poets to do this shit.
I was writing free verse poems when yaw thought
    if it didn't rhyme it was a speech and shit
I was wearing ties & hard bottoms when yaw thought
    it was corny to dress like a grown man and shit
Follow me, take notes…

I write that other shit, get the panties from ya' mother
    shit, and infiltrate ya' memory bank, deep cover
    shit homie
You open mic nights; I'm opening up for fight night
    Mayweather MGM for 50 grand this scribe life
I never share my thoughts cause niggaz will steal ya'
    thoughts then look you in the face talking about
    it's something that they bought
I write the smartest shit,
    you need a dictionary to decipher it plus,
    I spit that up top northern slang def poet shit
I got metaphors that's straight up better than yours
    and I keep similes for niggaz who resemble me
You got show scribes, little to no scribes
    sell a bunch of books and you still owe scribes

I got full blown scribes that multiply to more scribes,
> I could die come back & write nine more
> scribes equivalent to my lives

Slick like a black cat and that's a natural fact,
> I will creep in ya' mix and give ya' bitch a poetic
> fix

And now y'all got these young poets all on the set
> acting like they're the laureate
> all in their dumb scribes writing nothing but lies
> and when they step on the stage
> I can see the fear in their eyes
> I can hear the fraudulence in their speech,
> so I question that of which they speak
> and they cred out in them streets

Y'all wanna be poet ass niggaz y'all funny to me,
> writing ya own scribes but you still wanna be
> me I guess for every scribe you write I write
> 103 and you still running around thinking
> you got something on me, but I been wrote it

Y'all wanna take my scribes and run with them
> that's ok just know they got the copyright with
> them

I'm thee Original, the laureate of my time,
    but I will still bust down yo' hoe with the coldest
    of rhymes and ride for mines when the shit
    gets critical there are no lies in these lines
    please take these words literal
Groupies I leave them fucked, these poets all stuck
    and if you think your fucking with me, HA
    good luck
Last year they had no fear this year they should be
    terrified because I'm coming with metaphors &
    entendres they can't deny
Poets keep crying, but Pure Titan keep grinding
    and while they all complaining
    I keep writing more diamonds,
    rocking more Steve Madden no NFL,
    I keep some hard bottoms on my feet
    to stomp these fake poets to hell

Don't believe me if you want I'll leave all you
    muthafuckas slumped in a trunk from poetical
    bars because my wordplay is like Sars
    or something similar to taking a walk on
    Mars… deadly

It's crazy how one scribe can change the game
      and even with a 4.0 I always want more brains
Ain't no entendres in ya' scribes while you writing a
      mile high you better step up ya' game
Ain't no knowledge on board you better switch ya'
      plane

Scornful Intentions

The opening in your chest I put there and could care
    less, I wanted to rip out your heart,
    my only regret is not getting a chance
    to step on it after I tossed it to the wayside,
    fuck you and everything you believe in

I never had intentions on making you
    anything more than what we were, baby
    you knew what this was when you met me

The dream I sold you was manufactured in a
    nightmare plant I learned what you wanted,
    needed, & expected so I conformed to all of
    thee above
I noted your fears and all the things you didn't want
    and never wanted to experience
I lured you in & took advantage of your heart
I exploited your fears and made them my goals,
    which resulted in your downfall
I met you hating you... entranced by your beauty
    & captivated by your booty, but repulsed by
    your attitude and sickened by your voice

Sweetheart I've turned away badder bitches then you,
    but your arrogance intrigued me
    making you my personal project
    and you ain't even have a clue
I poured ambrosia on your lips and tainted it with hatred

Your Swag

You say it's your swag
    I say it's my allure
You think I'm drawn to you?
Think back sweetheart,
    you said hello to me, but you licking ya' lips
    & switching ya' hips I did indeed see
Walking by with your head held high
    cutting ya' eyes & smiling at me

You say it's your swag
    I say it's my hypnosis
The reason why I'm still screaming pimp or die
You think I'm tryna make a love connection,
    but all I want is for your "love" and my "love"
    to get connecting
Yeah I do flowers & yeah I do candy,
    but please believe in my back pocket
    that golden delight is handy
I don't do motels, only 5 star hotels
    that keep my line of groupies as long as the
    Nile, but only a select few do I keep on speed
    dial… your # 22 send

You say it's your swag
> I say it's my charming wit

I look at other girls because they be sexy as shit,
> but girl you know I only got eyes for you
> & I only smile when I say that cause I'm thinking about the other seven girls I said that to

Of course I love the way you walk,
> cause you thick as a brick

Of course I love the way you talk,
> cause you freaky as shit & no I don't be hanging on ya' words, I be looking at ya' tits

I never wanted to impress you,
> just put it on you

Your swag, more like your liability

My swag
> Effective
>
> Forceful

I am man
> hard, never soft
>
> silly, yet smart

That's your liability
> that has you falling apart

VENTING

My mind is playing tricks on me, I think
    or at least I hope it is
Confusion and fear are my only emotions
    confused as of why,
        but secretly knowing the reason
In fear of the legion of sins I committed
    has come for their pound of flesh
I'm pissed at this bitch and I wanna be justified,
    but fearful that if I speak up
    I'll find her emotions have died
How dare you expect me to sit and wait,
    knowing my sexual appetite is as if I never ate
Insatiable is the word that comes to mind
    and complete satiation is what I tried to find

No call, but you book?
No text, but you tweet?
I was shocked to see you showed up,
    but was hurt when you didn't speak
Bitch I loved you, but you left me and didn't care,
    those tears you cried put some in mine,
    but now my tear ducts are bare

I only had two tears anyway,
    one for each eye and I feel like
    I wasted them on you, now becoming an
    emotionless monster is the only thing left to do
No emotions, no feelings, no heart... FUCK IT
    I guess I'm gonna be trife forever,
    a different chick in my life every night forever,
    in fact, I prefer two together and get high
    to balance the lows I may be feeling forever
I asked God to give me Army strength,
    to make me strong, so I could carry the
    burdens you've endured for so long, but you
    left
I realized being army strong is just a cliché,
    since that's where you'd rather be
    instead of with me to stay
For pain I don't have the patience,
    so I suffer silently and fake my elation
Damn, I wish we would've had that conversation,
    the one where you mentioned your motives
    and I told you I hated them so we could have
    parted ways by choice before we parted ways
    by force
Fuck uncle sam and everybody that loves him!

Barhead Geese

Tryna grab a beach
    and build a crib on it homie
    because that's not out of my reach
Attempting to make this earth for my kids
    something similar to heaven,
    looking out of plane windows thanx to 747, Inc
    don't you think for one second shit sweet,
    get caught slipping in my city guaranteed you'll
    feel the heat
What do you think, your like me?
    I'm not your rival I'm your idol,
    next to the definition of what you wanna be
    is a picture of me chilling with all the
    championship belts blowing on hydro and that
    is word to Michael Phelps
Catch me swimming in women that's down with so
    much sinning they never make it to my bed
    linens
Shark shit
    dissolves like the panties on these bitches
    when they tryna steal a glimpse of my riches

Hopping on a flight
Flying high above the clouds
Barhead Geese can't see what I see

Pearling dutches back to back in all black
Barhead Geese can't see what I see

Wannabe poets can't measure up and they know it
Barhead Geese can't see what I see

Scribing my life they hate cause they know it ain't fake
Barhead Geese can't see what I see

Tryna come up writing scribes for my crew,
    that's what I wanna do
Flights nigga… Co-founder of a dope coalition,
    telling bitches I'll see them when I see them
    cause right now I'm on a mission
Yet they still wishing for the best position
    next to me to flex with me
    to spend my bread and smoke my tree,
    praying for a free ride to the top with me,
    but it cost to be the boss so I let them take
    a ride on me that they think is free

then charge an extra fee so they come put that
    top on me
Looking fly as ever, will I drop homie never,
    she not answering because your bitch in my
    passenger sliding on that butter soft leather
Catch me in the middle of PA in Coatesville scribing in
    the clouds getting my thoughts together
    preparing for another endeavor
    to go toe to toe with whomever
    & crush a hater who hating cause my scribes
    more clever

Hopping on a flight
Flying high above the clouds
Barhead Geese can't see what I see

Pearling dutches back to back in all black
Barhead Geese can't see what I see

Wannabe poets can't measure up and they know it
Barhead Geese can't see what I see

Scribing my life they hate cause they know it ain't fake
Barhead Geese can't see what I see

Risky

She came first I came last then we rolled the grass
    I hit it a few times and dove back on that ass
When we link we usually put up 3 or 4 but this time
    we were on a time limit because her man was
    just running out to the store
That is the risk we'll take since we both been home
    feeling like fiends locked in with our families
    during this quarantine
Them lines in the store be popping so we have time to
    finish, because bull gonna be gone for about
    45 minutes
By the end of the session I was calling her Robin
    because she was given everything I came
    for and in just under 42 minutes I was back out
    the door but I almost got stuck because after
    we put one up I got two n she got three nuts
See it was a must that we released our quarantined
    lust so when back locked in with the fam there
    ain't no fuss yeah we both have people at
    home that we do more than bone and if they
    knew about this they definitely wouldn't
    condone

I could have never foreseen that during quarantine
    to keep the peace and to say the least
    I had to get me a Corona free side piece

I Love Being A Poet

I got a real poetic face and a real poetic smile
    I got a real poetic flow and a poetic style and in
    my lifetime I flipped a million worth of vowels
Poets thinking I'm sweet because I haven't been on
    the scene in a while, but this work gon' speak
    for itself so I just sit back and smile
A nice guy I haven't had to get dark in a while,
    but my mind will make a brother question
    if I was ever on a quest for love or my black
    thoughts go deeper than the very roots of me
    which would mean most definitely
The day I lay my soul is here and through words and
    phrases I present it to the masses like it's
    magic or maybe Badu I meant voodoo
    while giving you all a window seat to the show
If back then moms knew I was writing this much crack
    she would've kick me to the curb for having it in
    her house and since it's real in the field I keep
    the notebook in the wheel in case I gotta load
    the pages and kill and tho I'm in it for the art
    I'd love to make a mil

Whether it's your girl or opportunity this poet, ima take
    that talk crazy and these bars will have you
    and that shit your on floating where the lake at
It's Pure Titan creeping where yo momma and yo
    aunty at and if they never been with melanin
    you know they never going back
Coatesville dude putting in work like them hard hats
    type voice that'll make your lady want to run
    these bars bars back
I'm putting books on the shelves so everybody can
    read that and no I ain't James Brown but know
    this is the payback

Complexion 4

Syne

"Acting on these feelings of passion and wanting to take you, desire and wanting to hear you, lust and wanting to taste you."

Anytime Anyplace

In the thunder & rain
    I stare into your pages
I can feel your smooth texture
    underneath my hand, baby it's like you're
    ageless
Pencil in my hand
    takes me to another land
I can feel your spirals
    Hhmmmm damn

I could never stop just because
    people showing up & watching us
I could care less what they think
I want to write now
I could never stop just because
    Poetry baby you are my love
I'm not gonna stop oh hell no
I want to write, so all I'm gonna say is
Anytime and anyplace
I'll write my thoughts down &
    I don't care who's around

Sitting in the park with the wind blowing over my waves my mind is on 1000, baby I am your slave
Eyes peeking all around, but I never keep you face down, face up I spread you wide
so strangers can admire what's inside
Under the rays of the sun or down low we turn the lightsI was thinking maybe I could well, you know... write

I could never stop just because
people showing up & watching us
I could care less what they think
I want to write now
I could never stop just because
Poetry baby you are my love
I'm not gonna stop oh hell no
I want to write, so all I'm gonna say
Anytime and anyplace
I'll write my thoughts down &
I don't care who's around

Chocolatey Thoughts

There is a certain allure emitted from chocolate
    women, so when they meet my eyes they take
    complete dominion
Sovereign ruler of my thoughts
    and at one point I thought I could resist their
    reign, but that was a fleeting thought, because
    the harder I fought the deep I feel into
    servitude & obedience

I swear the first time I kissed a chocolate woman
    I tasted some of her ingredients
A couple cups of attitude, gallons of strength,
    a few liters of courage and perseverance
    and a quart of aggression to add to the
    experience
Yes there was some sugar and also some spice,
    but they made not even the top ten of
    ingredients that made her taste so right
Mother of me, mother of my children, mother to the
    world I am indebted to them and my allegiance
    can not be bought, but these are just some of
    chocolatey thoughts

Stormy Weather

Yes I admit, I wanted to make you an addict
So I became the exemplary figure
    of all my positive attributes;
    all that you like, all that you admire,
    all that you love about me
    became every inch of my flesh
    and every ounce of my blood
I would watch you slip into day wonders
    as we conversed over how long I would stay,
    which was long enough for me,
    never long enough for you,
    always long enough to bring pleasure,
    yet never long enough for you to get
    comfortable, but just long enough to keep you
    wanting, which would turn into a craving,
    then evolve into a yearning for... me
Knowing with an arrogant mind frame
    that I was your weak spot
So I admit, I wanted to make you an addict

You were my earth's terrain,
    as it never took long to make you wet

Complete saturation is what it was
A swirling vortex of wind is what I enraptured you in
    as I romanced you
Becoming a cumulonimbus cloud,
    I would explore your upper atmosphere
    soon to become magma
    and flow through your inner core
Causing dormant volcanoes to become active,
    rumbling on the verge of eruption
Becoming arctic wind, blowing and sending shivers
Becoming black sand clinging to your mental,
    serving as an aphrodis-I need some raindrop
    kisses
Pushing your thinking, reasoning, and logical
    processes to the limit
Causing confusion, you struggle to understand,
    but you can't your mind is pulsating
    to every second to the flash of a solar flare
You were always so elated when I came around,
    you would dance and do all the things you do
You could sense my presence like the scent of rain
    ever so lightly frolicking on the midnight air
You become amazingly infatuated with the weather
    watching, wishing, and waiting for... it

Troubles & doubts melted away
    as the flames of relief blazed
Only during certain day wonders and dream filled
    sleepless nights would I cascade in on a
    shooting star, bringing with me a whirlwind of
    tongue, hurricane hands and spine tingling
    snow filled kisses

I wanted to make you an addict
    so I could watch you slip into day wonders
    as I acknowledge your physical
Easing away the hex of troubles & doubt
Knowing with an arrogant mind frame
    that I was your weak spot
It's calm within me I am the eye of the storm
I just thought I'd tell you why I made you an addict
    because it's trouble to neither of us
P.I.E.C.E to me
P.E.A.C.E of mind
Loved being your darkness
Always knew when to strike
Lighting
Strong Winds
Thunder

Streams of magma
Because I fell in love with your desires instead of
    your needs
Your body whispers the forecast to me,
    so you can wish upon this shooting star
    and make your dreams come true

Real Thing—Wish Granted

Acting on these feelings of passion
    and wanting to take you
Desire and wanting to hear you
Lust and wanting to taste you

A thought of you lovingly overwhelms my mind
Gently caressing every inch
    of your beautifully crafted heavenly body
Raspberry kisses to your frontal lobe,
    nibbles on your ears and more kisses
    to your lips, neck, breast, thighs
    and everything in between
Remain down,
Ecstasy

To receive the full effect of this seduction
    of every time, the vision of us intertwined
    enters and over comes your mind of the matter
    and completely overtakes the chemistry
    in the pit of your body
Because every time I enter physically,
    questioning stops and the definition of your

    pleasure rises up in the form of moans and
    plates of vertebrae chills
Touching every wall
Creating laughter and making love,
    anticipating the ultimate climax

Ascending with every stroke
New levels to every position
Anyway I want you, I have you
    loving the heights I take you to
    in order to maximize this seduction
    while caressing every inch of you
    inside and out
No longer a prototype, yet only for one night.

Desire & Confess

I have a confession to make
I got this yearning
    that can only really be described as a craving
    which if I'm totally honest with myself
    can only truly be described as an obsession
    and if I wanna be truly honest about
    being totally honest I must say that
    my confession is more of a divine revelation
Which is you're my guilty pleasure

A shameless dichotomy worshiper of you I am
An admirer of your stature I am
Amazed by your grace I am
    constantly indulging in day wonders
    about your embrace hoping that it's not a sin
Woman of surprise
Woman of mystery
Woman of beauty
    that precedes the pages of history
The regality of Cleopatra
    with the leadership and compassion
    of Mother Teresa herself

Making such a woman
> more valuable than the composite
> of any amount of wealth

As I sit and reminisce
> over the countenance of our endeavors

I must confess that you're my guilty pleasure

Mounting passion resulted in days of wonder
> and nights of lust with hours of conversation
> saturated with pure seduction

Drip... Drip... Drip

Star filled skies
> serve as a natural aphrodisiac

So gaze my bedroom nymph gaze

Imagination's flaring,
> creating new ways
> to explore each other mentally

There's a certain mentality
> involved with orchestrating this symphony

I can hear the notes and see the melodies
> your body plays for me

Baby you're my music
> and as the song of life is being strummed

by the chords of our duet,

the love making sounds are followed

to a place of forever

and while there I must confess

You're my guilty pleasure

Frustration

Him: Hello my love

Her: "Oh you talking to me, I didn't even realize that cause work, work, work, all you do is fucking work! I know you have things to handle, business to take care of, and an empire that you're trying to build, BUT DAMN! I'd swear if they weren't papers that you were having sex with them, because they are the only things you've been putting your hands on lately!" She yelled.

Him: "First off woman, watch your god damn mouth. Second, please relax with all this, you know I have too much going on right now to be arguing with you and not be focused on what I need to do to get things done. Can you not start with me today?" He pleaded.

Her: click

~10 minutes later via text~

Him: Where are you woman?
Her: Home, why?
Him: OMW, be there soon so don't fucking leave!

Her temper is blazing, her thoughts are scrambled
    and her hormones are raging
She's talking to herself, yet talking to him
    and cursing him clean out although he's
    nowhere around for himself to defend
Mad is not her emotion sexual frustration is,
    so she sets off to the shower to handle her biz
    and for her temper to fizz
There is no doubt she can get what she wants,
    but what she needs is her man
    and despite what she thinks is the plans
    soon he'll be holding her in his hands
The shower is comforting,
    but only temporarily
After two go rounds with herself
    she was more hungry than ever
    and only a man, her man could fill her
Thoughts of riding him into an orgasmic coma
    runs rampid as she freed herself
    from the clutches of her temporary lover

He left the office in a hurry
    and although anger had his vision was blurry
    when he reached the driveway he calmed
    himself by talking to himself yet talking to her,
    whispering sweet nasty secrets and thinking of
    the faces she makes as he's deep in it
He steps out the car, loosens his tie,
    and opens his suit jacket
    knowing she can never deny,
    how good he looks fresh off the clock
    and when he steps into her world all
    questioning stops
No more, who's, how's, where's or why's,
    only truth, his insatiable sweet tooth
    and honey dripping from her hive

Only a towel adorns her splendid caramel body
    and as he peers through the window she does
    too
Eyes locked & temperatures rising
She dropped her gaze to his crotch,
    he dropped his gaze to a love moistened spot
They're both growing

She opened the door,
    he opens the screen and for a moment in time
    it all seems like a dream
He can see the steam rising off her body
    as the water droplets drip down her chest,
    glistening like a pearl necklace in the sunlight
One hand holds the door cracked catching the
    breeze, while his other removes her towel
    and her nipples plump with ease
The sight is such a tease that he wants to dive right in
    and in her most glorious state the feast can
    begin
In his arms she jumps with passionate kisses that
    follow, despite his schedule for today home is
    where he must stay so his evening meetings
    can be rescheduled for tomorrow
He attempts to cuff her ass for his pleasure
    & her stability, but stops realizing the extent of
    her agility with hands barely touching his face
    she's using only her legs to hold herself in
    place
A smile forms in his mind,
    yet a physical manifestation comes quickly
    behind

He let her down & stepped back to admire her body
    making a mental note to keep paying for her
    pilates
She takes advantage of the moment laying back on
    the rug, closing her eyes & contorting her body
    in an intriguing position that's screaming "take
    me now," and he's inclined to listen
Her unopened eyes missed him stepping out his
    Ferragamo loafers, taking off his suit jacket,
    tie, cufflinks, and shirt on the sly
By the time she opened them again to see the sun's
    rays there was none, only dark chocolate
    splendor met her gaze, he stood before her
    and the inevitable happened

Since You Say I May, You Know I Will

Take you in the a.m., before the hustle and bustle
    of everyday life takes hold
Before the morning worker reaches her vehicle
      to knock off the frost as she prepares for her
    daily commute
Before the fathers of the world put on their robe
    and cook breakfast for the children
    preparing them for their day of knowledge
I'll catch you in that moment of screaming silence &
    REM sleep, personifying your dreams
You're willing to give, so I ask
    if I may have some honey
The sweet rush of sensation
    is just what I need to get me going
A touch of heaven enraptured your being
    as my lips engulf yours disbursing the
    monotony from the most mundane of Mondays

You savor the flavor and I say
    physics has no hold over you
    as even when you're not in my presence
    on the tip of my tongue is where you stay

A sprinkle of sugar and a splash of spice makes
    everything nice, so show me what you're made
    of, do I have magic before me now?

The sounds of love are synonymous
    with the sensual moans of the wind
Your lips are inviting mines once again and you say,
    I may embrace your body
    and let my chocolateness dance over you
    creating euphoric shadows upon the walls
    and floors and chests of wood
Words have become obsolete
    as body language is the communication
    method of choice and the zone of love making
    is entered
Let the marathon begin

You acknowledge my intelligence and accept me for
    me, in return the adoration I have for you is
    unmatched as I worship your dichotomy
    shamelessly
You give, I take, you take and I say Since you say I
    may, you know I will

You Have One Job

They say there is somebody for everybody,
    so I question if that means somebody or
    somebodies because if there is really only one
    for me I'ma be pissed because a brother like
    me need two or three and that is a part
    of the flourishing master in me
I'm trying to take those steps to see
    how that is going to be because
    monogamy just ain't for me,
    but the word that rhymes and starts with p
    seems to be more reasonably ideal for me
    and all you gotta do is say yes

You have one job and that is to say yes,
    don't stress or allow yourself to be under
    duress just relax and undress and if you not
    saying yes than you should less, because you
    have one job

I love to make more than one woman mine,
    and making love to more than one woman
    can take some time

I recognize the hesitation in your eyes
        and it's not a surprise just know that I am
        obliged to keep you comfortable at all times
The veil of confusion will be lifted tonight
        and sense is going to be made tonight,
        so tonight all you gotta do is say yes

You have one job and that is to say yes,
        don't stress or allow yourself to be under
        duress just relax and undress and if you not
        saying yes than you should less, because you
        have one job

ACKNOWLEDGEMENTS

There are more people than I could fit on this page who I could thank for contributing to this moment. I have to thank God for the ability to create, this gift is beyond appreciated. My sister Jessica for helping me to cultivate this gift before I even knew it was one. Thank you to my Shmink for always reminding me how words can inspire. Without my parents Eric & Adgrian always having my back regardless of what was happening I definitely wouldn't be here today. H! My oldest son, you've pushed me more than you'll ever know, thank you my boy. Doug, you are my white knight, my angel & my #1 fan, thank you for everything. Peaches my Queen, without being able to bounce ideas off of you a lot of scribes would never have been created, I truly thank you. To the relationships & friends I acquired at Liberty University, thank you, so many of those situations and encounters were transformed into scribes. I could go on & on, but to my right hand, my brother, my best friend since the 2nd grade. Kev we are 22 years in and counting. You have inspired, pushed and supported me since it all started. This is just the beginning for us, may the odds and God's favor forever be on our side, SALUTE!

Published By Books Speak For You Publishing

Specializing In 7 & 21 Day Publishing

Publishing In Over 100 Languages

267-318-8933

Printed In The United States

www.booksspeakforyou.com

www.ingramcontent.com/pod-product-compliance
Lightning Source LLC
Chambersburg PA
CBHW071009160426
43193CB00012B/1981